HANDY HEALTH GUIDE TO SORE THROATS

Alvin and Virginia Silverstein
and Laura Silverstein Nunn

Enslow Publishers, Inc.
40 Industrial Road
Box 398
Berkeley Heights, NJ 07922
USA

http://www.enslow.com

Original edition published as *Sore Throats and Tonsillitis* in 2000.

Library of Congress Cataloging-in-Publication Data

Silverstein, Alvin.
Handy health guide to sore throats/ by Alvin and Virginia Silverstein and Laura Silverstein Nunn.
pages cm. — (Handy health guides)
 Summary: "An overview of what causes sore throats and other illnesses such as tonsillitis and strep throat"—Provided by publisher.
Includes bibliographical references and index.
 ISBN 978-0-7660-4279-7
 1. Throat—Diseases—Juvenile literature. 2. Tonsillitis—Juvenile literature. I. Silverstein, Virginia B. II. Nunn, Laura Silverstein. III. Title. IV. Title: Sore throats and tonsillitis.
 RC182.S3.S555 2014
 616.3'1—dc23
      2012045735

Future editions:
Paperback ISBN: 978-1-4644-0501-3
EPUB ISBN: 978-1-4645-1259-9
Single-User PDF ISBN: 978-1-4646-1259-6
Multi-User PDF ISBN: 978-0-7660-5891-0

Printed in the United States of America

052013 Lake Book Manufacturing, Inc., Melrose Park, IL

10 9 8 7 6 5 4 3 2 1

To Our Readers: We have done our best to make sure all Internet Addresses in this book were active and appropriate when we went to press. However, the author and the publisher have no control over and assume no liability for the material available on those Internet sites or on other Web sites they may link to. Any comments or suggestions can be sent by e-mail to comments@enslow.com or to the address on the back cover.

Enslow Publishers, Inc., is committed to printing our books on recycled paper. The paper in every book contains 10% to 30% post-consumer waste (PCW). The cover board on the outside of each book contains 100% PCW. Our goal is to do our part to help young people and the environment too!

Illustration Credits: Aaron Haupt/Science Source, p. 28; Biophoto Associates/Science Source, p. 19; BSIP/Science Source, p. 11; CDC, p. 18 (top); Daniel Kaesler/Photos.com (girl) Dr. P. Marazzi/Science Source, p. 27; Dynamic Graphics/Photos.com, p. 18 (bottom); Eye of Science/Science Source, p. 26; © iStockphoto.com/Christine Glade, p. 4; © iStockphoto/Jo Unruh, p. 42; © iStockphoto/Milorad Zaric, p. 14; © iStockphoto.com/Severin Schweiger, p. 8; © iStockphoto.com/yocamon, p. 40; Juanma García Escobar/Photos.com, p. 6; Juergen Berger/Science Source, p. 25; Jupiterimages/Photos.com, p. 37; PHANIE/Science Source, p. 10; Shutterstock.com, pp. 1 (medicine bottle, lozenges, tissues), 3, 9, 16, 17, 21, 23, 24, 29, 33, 38; Southern Illinois University/Science Source, p. 32; Stockbyte/Photos.com, p. 41; Thinkstock Images/Photos.com, p. 12.

Cover Photo: Daniel Kaesler/Photos.com (girl); Shutterstock.com (medicine bottle, lozenges, tissues)

CONTENTS

A sore throat can make you feel miserable.

1

MY THROAT HURTS

You wake up one morning and your throat feels a little scratchy. At breakfast, you have trouble swallowing your food. Oh no, you have a sore throat! You may be coming down with a cold.

A sore throat is often one of the first symptoms of a cold. In fact, colds are the most common cause of sore throats. But many other things can make your throat hurt. Your throat may get sore if you yell too much at a football game. Allergies can also make throats sore.

Most sore throats are not serious. They will go away in a few days to a week. But sometimes, sore throats turn out to be a warning that something harmful is happening inside your body. So how do you know when your sore throat is serious? Read on to find out.

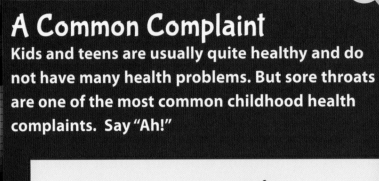

A Common Complaint

Kids and teens are usually quite healthy and do not have many health problems. But sore throats are one of the most common childhood health complaints. Say "Ah!"

2

WHAT IS THE THROAT?

Has a doctor ever told you to "Stick out your tongue and say 'Ah'"? The doctor wasn't really interested in seeing your tongue. He or she was trying to get a better look at your throat. Your throat can tell a doctor quite a bit about what's going on inside your body.

Shine a flashlight into your mouth and look at your throat in a mirror. Do you see the flap of tissue hanging down in the back? It looks like a punching bag. That is your uvula.

Behind the uvula is the entrance to your throat, or pharynx. Your pharynx is a tube that carries air to your lungs, food and drink to your stomach, and sounds from your vocal cords to your mouth.

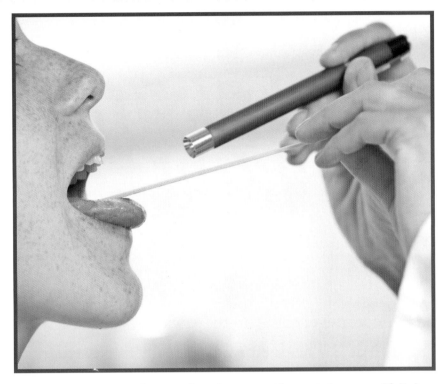

The doctor needs to check your throat to see if it is red and swollen.

As you look through the opening to your pharynx, you can see two large rounded blobs of tissue, one at each side. These are your tonsils. Healthy tonsils are pink, just like the rest of the throat. Although your tonsils are fairly large, they leave plenty of room for air and food to pass down the tube. When you get a cold or other illness, your tonsils may swell up. Sometimes they swell so much that they nearly close off your pharynx.

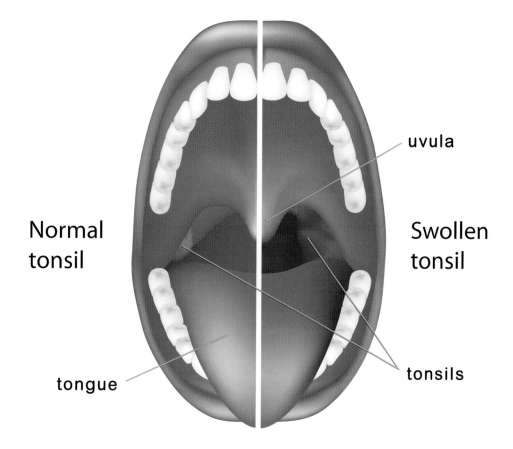

Normal tonsil

uvula

Swollen tonsil

tongue

tonsils

Open your mouth and look in a mirror. Can you see your tonsils, uvula, and tongue?

9

With the help of computer technology, a doctor can examine a patient's vocal cords right in the office.

You can't see it in the mirror, but your pharynx branches into two tubes leading down into the body: the air pipe, or trachea, and the food pipe, or esophagus. When you swallow, a leaf-shaped trap door called the epiglottis closes the opening to the trachea. It prevents liquid and food particles from going down your air pipe. Sometimes, usually when you eat too fast, the epiglottis

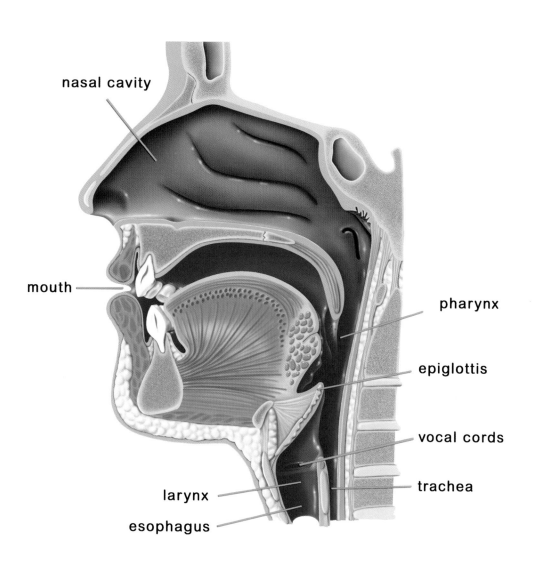

nasal cavity

mouth

pharynx

epiglottis

vocal cords

larynx

trachea

esophagus

Did you realize that your throat has so many parts?
The mouth leads to the pharynx, which continues
down to either the esophogus or the trachea.

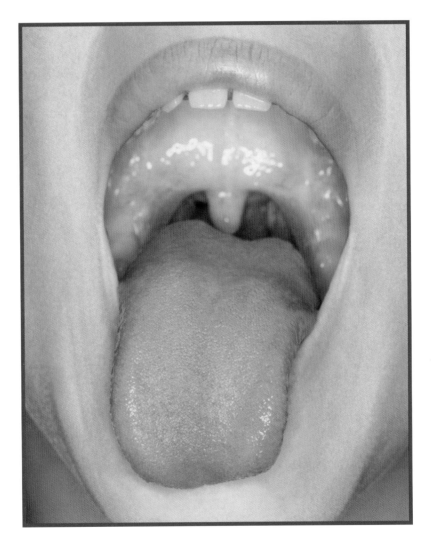

Take a look at the little punching bag—that is the uvula—at the back of this person's mouth.

does not close and something "goes down the wrong pipe." (When this happens, you probably have a sudden coughing fit.)

Look at your neck in the mirror while you swallow. Do you see a lump bulge out and move up and down? That is your voice box, or larynx. Your larynx is part of your trachea. There are two folds of tissue stretched out across your larynx. These are your vocal cords.

When your vocal cords are relaxed, there is a wide space between them, and air can flow through freely. When you talk or sing, your vocal cords move closer together. As air passes between them, they vibrate and make a sound. The thicker your vocal cords, the lower the sound they make. Women and children have shorter and thinner vocal cords than men. That's why their voices are higher than men's.

When You Can't Speak

Have you ever tried to talk, but no sound came out of your throat? That's what happens when you have laryngitis. When your larynx gets irritated and your vocal cords swell up, air has trouble moving between your vocal cords. You get laryngitis.

When just a little air can move between your vocal cords, you make sounds that are low, rough, and husky. You have a hoarse voice. Hoarseness is the most common symptom of laryngitis. Laryngitis may be the result of a cold, or may occur if you yell or cough a lot. Fortunately, laryngitis usually lasts only a few days.

3

WHY DOES MY THROAT HURT?

A sore throat may be a warning that you are doing something to hurt yourself. If your food or drink is too hot, it may burn the cells that line your mouth and throat. Burns can be really painful. Luckily, this kind of burn heals quickly. The damaged cells are soon replaced by healthy new ones. After a day or so, your throat won't hurt any more.

How can yelling give you a sore throat? Touch the inside of your mouth with your fingertip. Does it feel wet? The moisture inside your mouth and throat helps keep the cells that line them soft and flexible.

When you yell or scream, a lot of air moves through your throat. All that air carries away some of the moisture, and the lining starts to dry out. If the lining

Be careful! Don't burn your throat!

gets too dry, the cells on top may be damaged. This happens inside the pharynx, and it may also happen in your voice box. That is why yelling can make your throat sore—and your voice becomes hoarse.

In winter, the air inside most homes gets dry. Breathing all that dry air can dry your throat and make

Too much yelling and screaming can really make your throat dry.

it a bit sore. Breathing through your mouth, which you may do if your nose is stuffed up by a cold or an allergy, can also make your throat dry and sore.

All these things can give you a sore throat, but actually most sore throats are caused by an illness. When you get sick, your body is being attacked by germs. These germs are trying to get into your body's

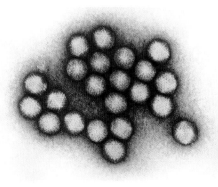

This adenovirus is one of the most common cold viruses.

cells, where they can get free food and shelter. They don't really mean to cause you harm. They're just looking for a cozy new home.

Everybody gets colds. They are called common colds because people get them so often. A cold is caused by a kind of germ called a virus. There are more than 200 kinds of cold viruses!

Handy Healthy Fact

Beware of Smoke

People who smoke often get sore throats. When they puff on a cigarette, they breathe in hot, dry smoke and irritating chemicals that can damage their throat. Have you ever had a sore throat after being in a room with a person who smokes? That's because some of the cigarette smoke was in the air you breathed.

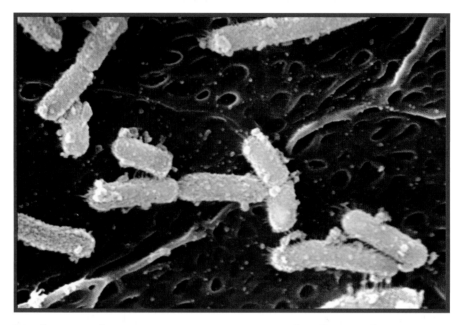

Under a microscope, you can see the bacteria, shown here in yellow, that live in the thin film that covers your teeth.

Viruses are so small that you can't see them even with an ordinary microscope. Scientists use high-powered electron microscopes to look at viruses. How small is a virus? If a virus were the size of an ant, you would be as big as the Earth.

Another kind of germ, called a bacterium, can cause illnesses that may give you a sore throat. Bacteria are much larger than viruses, but they are still too small to see without a microscope.

Activity 1: How Does Your Throat Get Dry?

Run the tip of your tongue over the roof of your mouth. It feels moist and slippery. Try pinching your nose closed and breathing with your mouth open for 30 seconds. What does the inside of your mouth feel like now?

Saliva, the watery fluid that constantly flows into your mouth, helps keep the lining moist. How does breathing through your mouth make it dry out?

To find out, wet two sponges and squeeze them out just enough so that they are not dripping. Place one sponge in front of a blowing fan. Place the other sponge away from the flow of air.

After five minutes, press a piece of paper towel gently against the surface of each sponge. Are both sponges still wet? If so, test them again after 10, 15, and 20 minutes. How long does it take for the surface of each sponge to dry out? How is this similar to what happened in your mouth?

You actually have bacteria living on your skin and inside your body. To see what bacteria look like, scrape off some of the material around the bottom of your teeth with a toothpick and look at it with a microscope. The bacteria look like little balls or sticks.

Most of the bacteria that live on or inside your body are harmless. For example, the bacteria in your intestines break down food so that you can digest it more easily. Some kinds of bacteria, though, can make you sick. One kind of bacterium makes an acid that eats away at your teeth and causes cavities. Another kind of bacterium, called streptococcus ("strep," for short), often attacks the throat. It causes an infection called strep throat.

Handy Healthy Fact

Viruses vs. Bacteria

Sore throats caused by bacteria, such as strep, can be treated with antibiotics—drugs that kill bacteria. But antibiotics don't work on common colds, which are caused by viruses.

4

THE BODY'S DEFENSES

When bacteria or viruses get inside your body, your body fights back. Some of the germs that enter your nose get trapped in bristly hairs inside your nostrils. Germs that sneak past these hairs fall into a gooey fluid that covers the lining of your nose. This fluid is called mucus. Mucus carries the trapped germs to the back of the throat. When you swallow, these germs—plus germs that have entered your mouth—travel to your stomach where they are destroyed in a pool of acid.

Other invading germs are destroyed by cells in your immune system. These special cells can identify foreign invaders—germs—that can harm your body. When viruses or bacteria attack your cells, those cells call for help. They do this by sending out chemicals that alert

What Is an Allergy?

Sometimes the immune system is a little too active. It mistakes something harmless, such as a food or pollen grains, as a threat. This is what happens in people who have an allergy. A sore throat may be the result of an allergic reaction. About 50 million people in the United States have allergies. That means one out of every five people is allergic to something. Do you have an allergy?

your immune system to the danger. It does not take long for an army of white blood cells to arrive. Like good soldiers, these cells identify invading germs and destroy them.

Some of the white blood cells make special chemicals called antibodies. They fit the virus, just as a key fits into a lock. Antibodies may kill germs, or they may make it easier for white blood cells to destroy them.

23

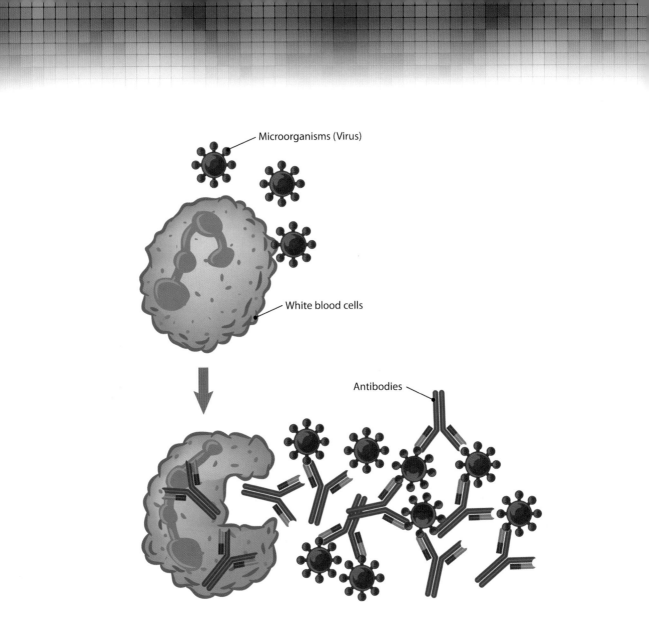

Microorganisms (Virus)

White blood cells

Antibodies

When viruses invade your body, some white blood cells produce antibodies. The antibodies attach to the viruses and help destroy them.

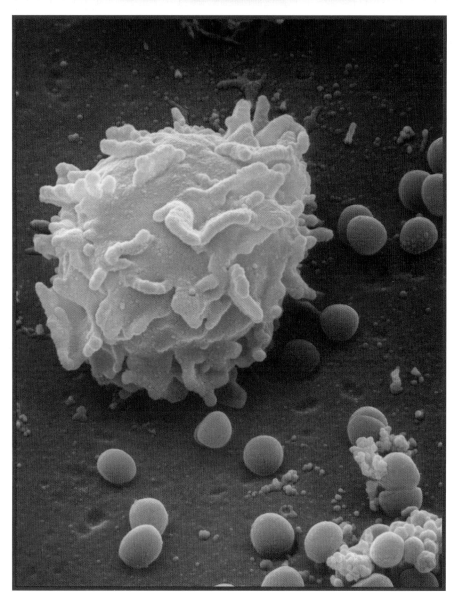

This image was taken through a microscope. The white blood cell (purple) is attacking a group of bacteria (red).

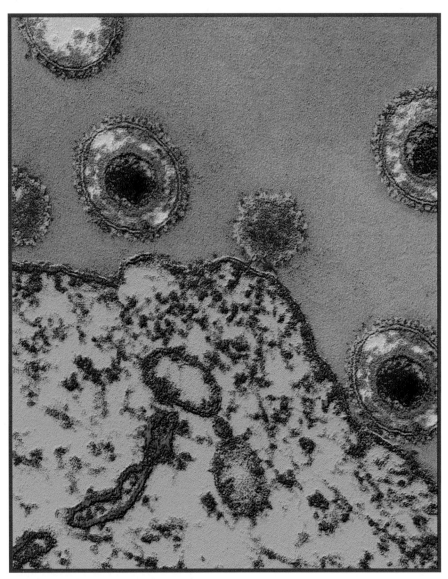

This image was taken through a microscope. It shows the chickenpox virus getting ready to attack a cell.

Once the body has made antibodies against the specific disease germs, it keeps some copies even after the illness is over. Then, if the same kind of germ invades your body again, the antibodies can quickly make a whole new army of antibodies to fight the invaders.

That's why you usually only get chickenpox or measles once in your life. If the germs that cause these diseases enter your body a second time, your antibodies destroy them right away—before they get a chance to make you sick. Fortunately, these days many people don't get these illnesses because they are vaccinated against them at a very young age.

Colds are a different story. There are so many different

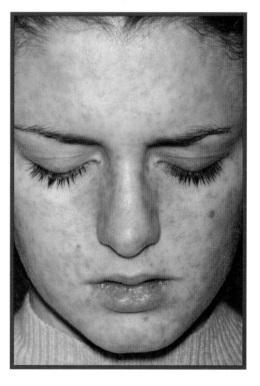

A sore throat may be a sign that you're coming down with measles. The characteristic spots show up a few days later.

kinds of cold viruses that when you catch a cold, chances are that it is not the same virus that made you sick the last time, or the time before that. That's why most people catch between 50 and 200 colds in their lifetime.

Your immune system works hard to protect you against invading disease germs, but it also causes some of the things that make you feel so miserable. Your body temperature rises, giving you a fever. The walls of the

Have you ever had a fever? When your body temperature rises, it means your immune system is working hard to fight disease germs.

Catching a Cold

Kids catch more colds than adults. Every time you have a cold, your immune system makes anti-bodies to fight the virus that causes it and saves some of them. That means you are protected. You won't get a cold caused by the same virus again. Parents and teachers catch more colds than most other adults because they're around children so much.

tiny blood vessels in your skin and throat lining get leaky. Fluid seeps out of the cells, and the area becomes red and swollen, or inflamed. When the lining of your nose swells, you have trouble breathing. Some of the fluid dribbles out, giving you a runny nose.

If particles of fluid get caught on the hairs in your nose, your brain sends a message to your chest muscles, and you sneeze. Some of the fluid drips down the back of your swollen throat and irritates it. The result is a sore throat.

5

WHAT IS TONSILLITIS?

For years, people believed that tonsils were useless blobs of tissue. They often became red and swollen when a person was sick, and seemed like easy targets for infections. If a person had tonsillitis (inflammation of the tonsils) several times, doctors usually took out the person's tonsils.

Doctors now know that your tonsils are a very important part of your immune system. These blobs of tissue are filled with special disease-fighting cells that trap invading germs and destroy them before they get a chance to reach the lungs. Many doctors believe that when the tonsils get red and swollen (inflamed), they are just doing their job. They are busy fighting germs.

What's That Stuff?

When tonsils become swollen and infected, they may have patches of white or yellowish pus. Pus is actually made up of dead white blood cells and germs.

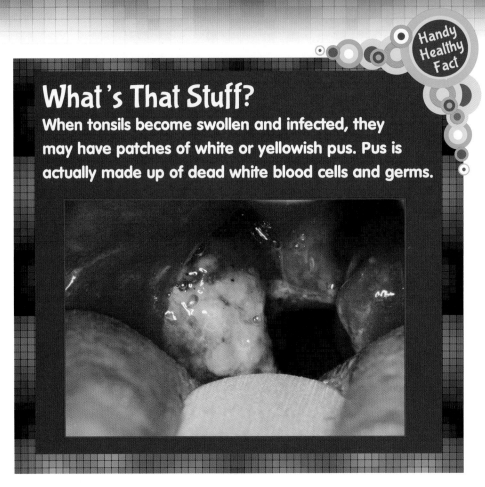

Nevertheless, people who get tonsillitis three or four times a year may need to have their tonsils taken out—especially if the tonsils swell up so much that it is difficult to eat and drink. When this happens, the tonsils are no longer helping the body. A tonsillectomy is a common operation today. The patient can usually go home the same day. After the operation, the patient's throat will be sore, and he or she will not be able to

After a tonsillectomy, you will need to eat soft food.

swallow solid foods for a while. Soft foods, such as gelatin or pudding, are good choices after having a tonsillectomy.

How do you know whether you have tonsillitis? If you do, your tonsils will look red and swollen and may have patches of white or yellowish pus. Your throat will be very sore, and you will have a hard time swallowing, especially when you eat or drink. You may also have a high fever, a headache, or an earache. If you have any of these problems for more than two to three days, you should see a doctor. When properly treated, tonsillitis goes away in a few days.

Tonsillitis can be caused by both viruses and bacteria, but most cases are caused by bacterial infections. An antibiotic can be used to treat the bacterial infections, but not the viral ones.

6

WHAT IS STREP THROAT?

Strep throat is an illness that often causes a sore throat, a high fever, and white or yellow patches on your tonsils or the back of your throat. Other symptoms may include red, swollen tonsils, a headache, stomachache, and swollen lymph nodes in the neck. (A doctor often checks the lymph nodes in the neck during an exam. Lymph nodes contain white blood cells and usually swell up when there is an infection.)

Strep throat is caused by group A *Streptococcus* bacteria. About 20 to 30 percent of all throat infections are caused by strep. Strep infections often lead to tonsillitis.

Strep throat is not easy to diagnose just by looking at a person's throat. The throat may look red and the tonsils swollen, but it may be just a really bad cold. Typically, a rapid strep test can be done right in the doctor's office. To do the test, a doctor or nurse wipes the back of your throat with a cotton swab. The swab picks up saliva and some of the bacteria on the lining of your throat. As its name suggests, the results come back very quickly—within 15 minutes! The test results show whether or not it's strep.

However, up to a third of those tested may get false results—that means that someone could actually have strep even though the test came back negative. If the test results do come back negative, the doctor may want to run a throat culture. A throat culture is more accurate than a rapid strep test, but the results take longer to come back—about two days.

If the rapid strep test or throat culture shows that you have strep throat, your doctor will want you to start taking an antibiotic right away. Most of the time, you will be able to go back to school the next day.

It is important to take all the antibiotic medicine that the doctor gives you. Don't stop taking it just because you start to feel better. When you do not take all of the medicine the doctor gave you, some of the bacteria may

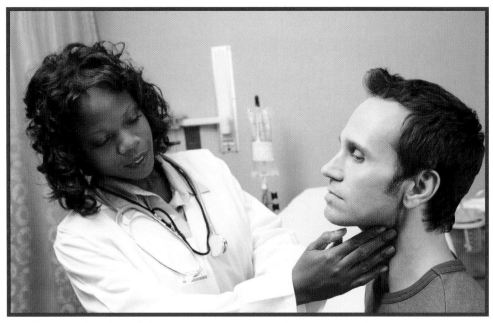

A doctor is checking this person's lymph nodes to see if they are swollen. If they are, he might have strep throat or some other illness.

survive and multiply. If these new drug-resistant germs are passed on to other people, they will not be helped by the antibiotic that made you feel better. After a while, that antibiotic may become useless for fighting strep infections.

When you have strep throat, your immune system makes antibodies to fight streptococcus bacteria. Some of the chemicals on these bacteria are similar to chemicals found in your joints and heart. If strep throat

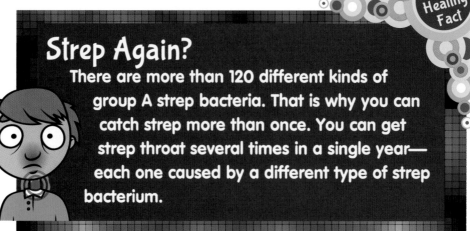

Handy Healthy Fact

Strep Again?

There are more than 120 different kinds of group A strep bacteria. That is why you can catch strep more than once. You can get strep throat several times in a single year— each one caused by a different type of strep bacterium.

is not treated, your antibodies may accidentally attack the cells in your joints and heart. This causes a disease called rheumatic fever. Rheumatic fever is not common in the United States, but someone with the disease runs a high fever and may have pain and swelling in the joints. The attacking antibodies may also damage the heart and kidneys.

7

HOW CAN I SOOTHE MY SORE THROAT?

Sore throats can be very painful, but there are several things you can do to make your throat feel better.

- Try to keep your throat moist. Run a humidifier in your home during the winter. When you fill a humidifier with water and turn it on, it changes the water into water vapor and pumps it into the air.

- Hard candy and throat lozenges can also soothe sore throats. They get the saliva flowing in your mouth and help keep your throat moist.

- Drinking plenty of fluids keeps sore throats from getting dry. Hot tea with honey can also have a

The steam from a humidifier helps to keep a sore throat moist.

soothing effect. Some medical experts tell their patients to gargle with warm salt water to help sore throats. (Add ½ teaspoon of salt to 1 cup of warm water.)

- Acetaminophen (an aspirin substitute) will also help to relieve the pain of a sore throat.
- Rest your voice. The more you talk, the drier your throat will become, and the more it will hurt.

Of course the best way to help your throat is to avoid getting sore throats in the first place. You can cut down on the number of sore throats you get by staying away from people with colds or strep throat. Do not touch any objects that they might have touched, either.

You should also do everything you can do to keep yourself healthy. Eat healthy foods, get plenty of sleep, and exercise every day. Wash your hands and shower regularly, wear clean clothes, and wash your food before you eat it. If your immune system stays strong, it will be able to fight off nasty germs.

Gargling a saltwater solution can soothe a sore throat.

Handy Healthy Fact

Activity 2:
Why Does a Dry Throat Hurt?

Start with two old, dry kitchen sponges. Try to bend one in half. Does it bend easily, or does it crack? Wet the other sponge, squeeze out the excess water, and try bending it in half. What happens?

The cells lining the mouth and throat are similar to a sponge. They need to be moist to stay flexible. If they dry out, they may crack when you swallow or talk.

Washing your hands regularly keeps you clean and healthy!

GLOSSARY

allergy—An overreaction of the immune system to a normally harmless substance, resulting in a sore throat, rash, sneezing, or other symptoms.

antibiotic—Medicine that kills bacteria.

antibody—A protein produced by white blood cells; some antibodies help to kill germs.

bacterium (plural bacteria)—A tiny living thing that is too small to see without a microscope; some bacteria cause diseases.

drug-resistant germ—A bacterium that is not killed by an antibiotic.

epiglottis—A leaf-shaped structure that closes off the trachea when liquids or solids are being swallowed.

esophagus—The food pipe; a tube that leads from the throat to the stomach.

immune system—The body's disease-fighting system; includes white blood cells, the lymph nodes, and the tonsils.

laryngitis—A swelling of the throat caused by an infection; it often causes hoarseness.

larynx—The voice box; a part of the trachea that contains the vocal cords and produces sounds when air passes through it.

lymph node—One of the small structures in the body that contain disease-fighting cells.

pharynx—The throat; the passage that leads from the mouth and nose to the trachea (air pipe) and esophagus (food pipe).

pus—Whitish or yellowish liquid in infected tissues, made up of dead white blood cells and germs.

rapid strep test—A fast-acting strep test that provides results within 15 minutes. Not as accurate as a throat culture.

rheumatic fever—An illness that may follow a strep infection; the immune system mistakenly attacks the body's own tissues and may damage the joints, heart, or kidneys.

strep throat—An infection of the throat lining by streptococcus bacteria; if untreated, it may develop into rheumatic fever.

throat culture—A test for strep throat.

tonsillectomy—Surgery to remove the tonsils.

tonsillitis—Inflammation of the tonsils.

tonsils—Two large blobs of tissue near the back of the throat.

trachea—The air pipe; a tube with muscular walls that leads from the throat to the lungs.

uvula—A flap of tissue that hangs down from the roof of the mouth at the entrance to the throat.

vocal cords—Two small folds of tissue that stretch across the larynx; air passing through the larynx makes them vibrate and produce sounds.

white blood cell—A cell that fights invading germs and other foreign substances.

LEARN MORE

Books

Brewer, Sara. *The Human Body: A Visual Guide to Human Anatomy*. London: Quercus, 2009.

Burgan, Michael. *Developing Flu Vaccines*. Chicago: Raintree, 2011.

Calamandrei, Camilla. *Fever*. Tarrytown, N.Y.: Marshall Cavendish Benchmark, 2009.

Klosterman, Lorrie, *Immune System*. New York: Marshall Cavendish Benchmark, 2009.

Peters, Stephanie. *The 1918 Influenza Pandemic*. New York: Benchmark Books, 2005.

Web Sites

Discovery Fit and Health. *Human Body: Body Systems*. "Respiratory System." <http://health.howstuffworks.com/human-body/systems>. Click on "Respiratory System."

Nemours Foundation. *TeensHealth*. "Strep Throat." <http://kidshealth.org/teen/infections/bacterial_viral/strep_throat.html>

INDEX